Essential Question
How can we understand nature?

How Butterflies Came to Be

by Deborah November
illustrated by Gina Capaldi

Scene 1
The Old Man

Setting: Native American village

house

corn

Old Man: Children, everybody is getting ready for winter. The women are grinding corn. The men are fixing their houses.

2

Old Man: I am ashamed because winter always makes me sad.

Child 1: The flowers will lose their petals.

Child 2: The beautiful colors will go away. It will be cold.

basket

Old Man: I have an idea! I am going to keep the colors of summer!

Child 3: That idea shows wisdom!

Child 1: We will be able to enjoy the colors of summer!

STOP AND CHECK

What is the old man's idea?

cactus

4

Scene 2
The Special Basket

sunshine

Old Man: I will use my special basket. It can hold plenty of things.

Child 2: We will dash around the village and find colors to put in the basket.

Old Man: I will put this golden sunshine into my basket first.

blue sky

Old Man: I must not boast, but everybody will be happy when they see the colors.

Child 3: I think you should put a piece of the blue sky into your basket.

STOP AND CHECK

What did the old man put into his special basket first?

Scene 3
Collecting More Colors

pine needles

Child I: Let's add green pine needles!

Old Man: I need something white. I can get it from the cornmeal that the women are grinding.

Old Man: I love flowers. I will put some into my basket.

Child 2: The purple, red, and yellow flowers are bright and beautiful.

Child 3: The colorful flowers are the perfect things to collect!

flowers

dirt

Old Man: I will also put the rich black of the earth into my basket.

Child 3: This is a great victory! You saved the colors of summer.

Old Man: Everyone, look here and see what we have done.

Child 2: <u>Come</u> and see the colors we have collected!

Child I: Hurry! Run!

<u>Come</u> is an irregular verb. You do not add -*ed* to form the past tense. Find another irregular verb on this page.

Language Detective

STOP AND CHECK

What colors were the flowers that the old man collected?

10

Scene 4
Butterflies Are Born

butterflies

Child 3: You will not believe your eyes!

Village Person 1: What pretty butterflies!

Village Person 2: They are every color of the rainbow.

In Other Words   You will be surprised by what you see. En español: *¡No lo podrás creer!*

Village Person I: The butterflies are fluttering everywhere!

Child I: One butterfly landed on my ear. That tickles!

Village Person 2: One landed on my head! That feels funny.

Child 2: The beautiful butterflies make me so happy! I want to holler!

Child 3: You must feel proud!

Old Man: Thank you, child. I am bringing <u>joy</u> to the village!

> **In Other Words** great happiness. En español: *una gran felicidad.*

Child 1: See the colors! We <u>have</u> collected golden sunshine and blue sky.

Child 2: We have the green pine needles. We have the white cornmeal.

Child 3: We have the purple, red, and yellow flowers. We have the black from the earth.

Old Man: Can you see the similarities to the things in the basket?

Language Detective	<u>Have</u> is a helping verb. Find another helping verb on page 13.

Village Person I: Nature gives the butterflies their colors.

Village Person 2: They are beautiful!

Old Man: And that is how butterflies came to be.

STOP AND CHECK

What flew out of the basket?

Respond to Reading

Summarize

Use important details to summarize *How Butterflies Came to Be.*

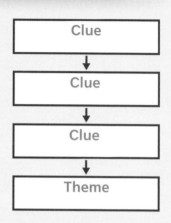

Text Evidence

1. How do you know *How Butterflies Came to Be* is a folktale? Genre

2. How does the old man collect all of the colors? Theme

3. Figure out what *fluttering* means on page 12 using root words. Root Words

4. Write about what you would put in the basket. Write About Reading

Compare Texts
Read a folktale about rainbows.

How the Rainbow Was Made

A man was walking in his yard. The yard had many flowers. One day, the man noticed that all of the flowers were white! He decided to paint the flowers. He used different colors.

flowers

Three birds flew into the man's yard.
They dipped their wings into the paint.
Then the birds flew high into the sky.

wing

paint

Rain fell from the clouds. The sun shone on the paint colors. The colors sparkled through the rain. There were red, orange, yellow, green, blue, and purple colors in the sky. And that is how the rainbow was made.

cloud

rainbow

Make Connections

How do stories help us understand nature? Essential Question

What does each tale explain about nature? Text to Text

Focus on
Literary Elements

Theme The theme is the life lesson or message in a story.

What to Look for Think about how the old man made the people in his village happy. What did he teach the people?

Your Turn

Imagine you are writing a folktale play about nature. Your play can teach a lesson. What details will you include? What part of nature will you explain? Make a list of your ideas.